**347**

# HANDEL: Concerto Grosso, Op. 3, No. 6

2 taps (½ measure) precede music.

SIDE A - BAND 1

PIANO

# HAYDN: Concertino in C major

## (Divertimento)

**3 taps (1 measure) precede music.**

SIDE A - BAND 3

1

Joseph Haydn (1732–1809)

347

8

2

**Menuetto**

(*la seconda volta p*)

Last time count in one.    (slightly faster)

## Trio

Fine    p

(la seconda volta p)

347

*Menuetto da capo*

**Allegro di molto**

# J. C. BACH: Concerto in B♭

SIDE B - BAND 1

Johann Christian Bach, Op. XIII Nr. 4

347

allow 15 seconds for Cadenza

8 Basso

**2 taps (½ measure) precede music.**

* The theme of this movement derives
from a Scotch popular song,
'The Yellow-haired Laddie'.

**MMO MUSIC GROUP, INC.** 50 S. Buckhout Street, Irvington, NY 10533